YULETIDE

Treasures

*Flowers, Garlands, and Trimmings
for a Merry Christmas*

Edited by John Beilenson

Design by Deborah Michel

Illustrations by James Henry

PETER PAUPER PRESS, INC.
WHITE PLAINS · NEW YORK

CONTENTS

INTRODUCTION

 he flowers, garlands, and greens we associate with a Merry Christmas have a long and sometimes ancient past. These symbols of peace, hope, and life everlasting often find their oldest roots in pre-Christian solstice celebrations.

Today, we bring wreaths and garlands, flowers and trees into our homes to usher in the spirit of Christmas. A tree decorated with antique bulbs, the piny scent of a potpourri, and the warm light of an Advent wreath remind us that Christmas is a time of thoughtfulness and kindness, of family and forgiveness, of good cheer and generosity to all humankind.

5

These Christmas trimmings also remind us of holidays past—baking cookies with our mothers, sewing felt Christmas stockings, waking up on Christmas morning. Today, families are busier than ever, but Christmas offers us a gentle reminder to slow down, to make the time for our sons and daughters, fathers and mothers, sisters and brothers.

Many of the recipes and holiday decorations included here can offer great opportunities to turn off the television and turn on the old-time Christmas spirit. Trimming the tree, teaching a son or daughter how to roast a turkey, taking a walk in some nearby woods (or even driving out to the store!) to gather a few evergreen boughs, sitting and reading Christmas stories—all these are wonderful moments to bring the holiday spirit into our homes and our families.

So, gentle reader, enjoy, and have a very Merry Christmas!

THE LANGUAGE OF
CHRISTMAS FLOWERS AND PLANTS

W hile many of us appreciate the aesthetic beauty of the holiday flowers and plants we use to decorate our homes, the rich and interesting histories of these blooms and evergreens are often forgotten.

For example, our tradition of bussing under the mistletoe actually derives from ancient Europe. When warring armies found themselves beneath an oak covered with mistletoe, they would declare a day of peace. The plant thus became a symbol of conciliation to which we have added our own more affectionate rituals. In the following section, you will find similar stories that can add a spiritual and festive significance to the sight and scent of these Christmas flowers and plants.

Ivy (Fidelity)

An attractive rope for Christmas wreaths and trimmings, ivy has survived its scandalous reputation as the signature plant of Bacchus, the Roman wine god. Until the last few centuries, Christians banned the vine from inside their homes, allowing it to grow only on the outside walls.

Holly (Foresight)

Perhaps the best-known of the Christmas greens, holly was first an invitation to jolly spirits to enter the pagan home during the cold winter months. Later, it stood as a symbol of Christ's life—the white flowers for His purity, the sharp, pointed leaves for His crown of thorns, and the bitter bark for His agony on the Cross.

Mistletoe (Healing and Goodwill)

Believed to have healing powers and long regarded as the "plant of peace," mistletoe held important meaning for Druid and later Northern European cultures. Today, we hang it in our homes to symbolize goodwill and to encourage displays of festive affection.

Hawthorn (Hope)

The Glastonbury (haw)thorn blossoms twice a year, in the Spring and around the Day of Epiphany. English lore relates the plant to the arrival of the missionary Joseph of Arimathea, who had placed his staff on the ground on the spot where the thorn first took root.

Rosemary (Remembrance)

A sweet-smelling addition to any Christmas wreath, rosemary's deep lavender bloom is the subject of a Spanish legend. While resting with the Baby Jesus, Mary placed her purple robe over a rosemary bush, which previously boasted white blooms—magically transforming the flower.

CHRISTMAS ROSE (LOVE)

Once called "Christ's herb," the Christmas Rose was believed to cure gout and relieve cholera. Today, it is still loved for its semi-annual blooms—the first of which is often on the very Day of Epiphany.

POINSETTIA (REVERENCE)

The "flower of the Holy Night" came to the United States in the 19th Century, courtesy of U.S. Ambassador to Mexico Dr. Joel Roberts Poinsett. According to Mexican lore, a poor stable boy traveling with the Three Wise Men on the night of Christ's birth had no gift for the Baby Jesus. He prayed contritely, and when he arose, a poinsettia miraculously grew. The boy took the vermilion blooms into the manger as an offering.

Laurel (Glory)

Hung today on doors as a friendly seasonal greeting,
laurel wreaths, like many evergreens of the season, also
celebrate the everlasting life Christ's coming signifies.

Cherry Blossom (Knowledge)

In Central Europe, people bring cherry branches indoors
at the beginning of Advent, place them in water, and by
Christmas have cherry blossoms blooming throughout the
house. Legend also has it that if a woman tends a sprig so
that it flowers on Christmas Eve, she will be married in
the coming year.

WREATHS

Laurel and other evergreen wreaths are lovely and sweet-smelling additions to a holiday home. Placing them on your front door makes a warm Christmas welcome for your guests in this festive season. But wreaths need not be consigned to the outside of the house. An indoor window wreath or a more modest table-top one can help fill the house with a fresh piny scent.

ADVENT WREATH

Advent wreaths, which should be placed where everyone can see them, are meant to serve as a reminder that Christmas is coming. On the four Sundays before Christmas, an additional candle or light is lit until Christmas Eve, when a large, center candle creates a warm and glowing sight on one of the longest nights of the year.

     The following are a few easy ideas to give your wreaths a special something extra.

DELLA ROBBIA WREATH

Form several thicknesses of wire into a wreath and fasten wires together. Wash and dry the most perfect fruits you can find. Lacquer or varnish thoroughly, and attach a wire stem to each fruit. Fasten to wreath at interesting intervals, interspersed with holly or other greenery. Lemons, oranges, tangerines, apples, and pears make a handsome large-fruit wreath, and cranberries, crabapples, and nuts make a good small-berry wreath. If you use walnuts, you might want to spray-paint them gold or silver.

Theme Wreath

Fasten miniature musical instruments, toys, animals, or other figurines such as doves or angels to a store-bought wreath. Small bells on a door wreath add a little jingling spirit every time someone comes inside the house. Bows and matching ribbons in holiday red or green or another favorite color brighten any festive display. Pine cones or even shells collected during the previous summer—spray-painted or au naturel—make nice additions too.

CHRISTMAS PROJECTS FOR THE WHOLE FAMILY

Making Christmas decorations can be fun for the entire family—a chance to spend quality holiday time with your young loved ones. Here are a few projects that will bring your family together and add holiday cheer to your home!

21

Christmas Potpourri

Our favorite bowl of Christmas potpourri is a redolent mixture sure to please the senses and waft the spirit of a traditional Christmas throughout the rooms of your home.

> *1 quart fragrant pine needles*
> *1 dozen small pine cones*
> *1 cup bay leaves*
> *1 cup bayberry leaves*
> *3 cups sassafras leaves*
> *3 cups orange peel*
> *1 cup cinnamon sticks*
> *1/2 cup whole cloves*

Make this recipe by the (dry) gallon, as it is popular and often disappears by the basketful. Children can help gather needles and cones. Brown needles or fresh green ones may be used. If the needles are very long, they can be cut, by the handful, to about two inches in length. Cones, if larger than a teacup, may be incorporated after other ingredients are mixed.

Bay leaves and bayberry leaves may be left whole. Use oak, magnolia, orange, or holly in place of, or in addition to, the sassafras leaves. Tree leaves are used fresh or dry, with about half of them crushed or broken at the time of mixing.

Save and dry orange and other citrus peels throughout the year for the potpourri. Cinnamon sticks broken to three-inch lengths or less, and whole cloves, complete the recipe!

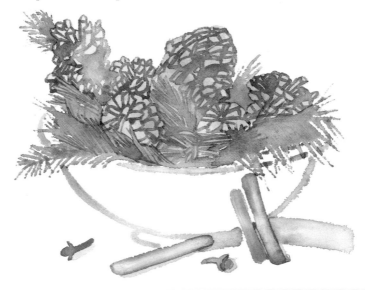

Spicy Pomanders

This is an excellent way to keep little fingers busy with really spectacular results.

Cover the surface of a thin-skinned orange with cloves, thrusting them in up to their heads. Roll in a mixture of orris root and cinnamon until orange is well covered. Wrap in tissue paper and put aside for one week.

At the end of the week, remove the orange from the tissue and shake off excess powder. Top pomander with a satin bow affixed to wire that is inserted into the pomander.

Pomanders are wonderful in linen closets or lingerie drawers and last for years.

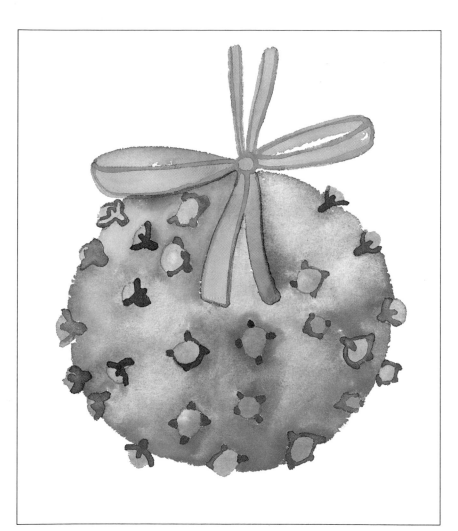

Vinegars with Verve

Cooks will love these herbal vinegars. Decorative and useful, they make wonderful gifts.

Sterilize some interesting bottles by boiling them for 5 minutes. Drop in each bottle three or four sprigs of either tarragon, ruby basil, sage, or thyme. Heat white-wine vinegar to 120° and pour into bottles. Seal tight with a cork or bottle top. Add a colored ribbon around the neck of the bottle, and you have a gift to be relished.

BIRDS' AND SQUIRRELS' CHRISTMAS TREE

Your children will have a lot of fun fitting out a backyard tree for their favorite outdoor friends! Choose a small fir tree, a branch of a tree, or a fine full bush and hang it with nuts, bread, suet, and stale cake, using leftovers of brightly colored yarn. A few colorful plastic balls will make the feeding station more festive in appearance and will withstand a week of cold weather.

GINGERBREAD HOUSE

On a cold, grey afternoon, when it's not nice enough to be outdoors, you can keep the children occupied helping to make a Gingerbread House. This recipe is easy. Just remember to have all the ingredients assembled in advance, so the children's attention won't wander!

> *3 boxes (14 ounces each) gingerbread mix*
> *3 cups water*

ROYAL ICING

> *1 box (16 ounces) confectioners sugar*
> *3 large egg whites*
> *1/2 teaspoon cream of tartar*

TO DECORATE
Choice of:

> *Strings of red or black licorice*
> *Gum drops, large and/or small*

Colored M & M candies

Life Savers

Jelly beans

Candy canes

Rectangular, light colored cookie for door

Food coloring to tint icing, if desired

Almond paste or marshmallow for chimney or
   snowman

Small sprigs of greenery

Preheat oven to 350°. For a base for the house, cover large piece of cardboard with aluminum foil and set aside. Empty 2 packages gingerbread mix into large bowl. Add 2 cups water and beat until well combined. Pour into ungreased 9 x 5-inch loaf pan. Bake 30 minutes or until top springs back when lightly pressed. Remove pan from oven but don't turn oven off. Place pan on rack and cool 10 minutes. Remove cake from pan and place on prepared cardboard or large platter.

     To make roof, empty remaining package gingerbread mix into bowl. Add remaining 1 cup water and beat until well combined. Pour into ungreased 11 x 7-

inch baking pan. Bake 20 minutes or until top springs back when lightly pressed. Place pan on rack and cool 10 minutes. Remove cake from pan and cut in half lengthwise. Trim edges if necessary.

To make icing, combine sugar, egg whites, and cream of tartar in large bowl of electric mixer. Beat at high speed until thickened. Icing should be used immediately to keep it from drying out. Keep covered with moist kitchen towel while working.

To assemble house, spread small amount of icing on 1 side of both halves of roof. Icing will serve as "glue." Position both halves, icing on the inside, at right angles to each other on top of house to make slanted roof. If necessary, use toothpicks for additional support.

Decorate gingerbread house as illustrated or in any way you choose. Spread white icing on roof for snow. Outline roof with licorice strings and decorate with candy. Tint small amounts of remaining icing red or green and pipe on house to outline door and windows. If cookie is used to make door, spread small amount of icing on inside of door to make it stick to house. Cut large gum drops in half and attach with toothpicks to make windows. Shape a small chimney out of almond paste or marshmallow, tint, and secure to roof. Add sprigs of

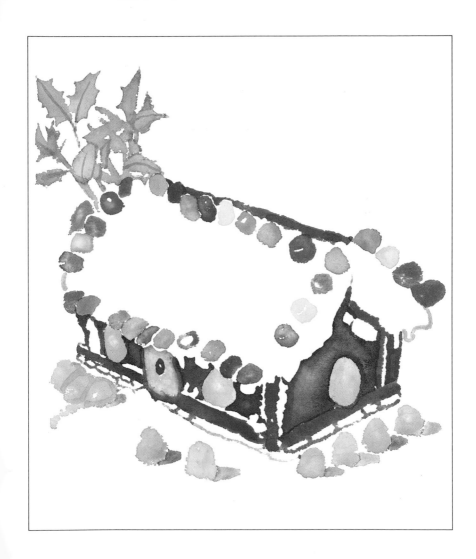

greenery to outside of house for shrubbery. If desired, spread white icing on aluminum foil around house for snow, or tint icing green for grass. Outline path to house with black licorice strings. Use small pieces of marshmallow and toothpicks to make miniature snowman. Or, best of all, let the children be creative.

More than Tinsel, Better than Bulbs: Great Tree Ideas

Bored with bulbs? Tired of tinsel? Here are a few ways to give your tree a new and interesting look.

35

DRIED FLOWERS

Hydrangeas, thistle, statice, or any of your favorites may be incorporated into a country classic tree arrangement.

NUTCRACKER TREE

If your house is filled with budding ballet dancers, a tree festooned with felt bows, bells, wooden soldiers, and sugarplums is sure to be a hit.

ECO-TREE

Environmentally conscious? Use recycled paper to make flowers and other tree decorations or even entire table trees. Make sure to recycle or compost the tree when you're done.

Empty-The-Kitchen-Drawers Tree

Use cookie cutters, candy molds and other festive kitchen utensils to cook up a special holiday tree.

Angel Tree

Adorn your tree with angels and cherubs for a heavenly Christmas.

Kitty in the Tree

For all you cat lovers, try decorating your tree with an assortment of stuffed or clay kitties for that purrrfect tree.

PC Tree

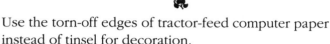

Use the torn-off edges of tractor-feed computer paper instead of tinsel for decoration.

Christmas Card Tree

Fasten the Christmas cards you receive to various branches so you will be reminded of your friends throughout the Christmas season.

The Edible Tree

Originated by Queen Victoria and King Albert in 19th Century England, a tree festooned with treats such as popcorn, cookies, dried fruits, and candy makes for an old-style Christmas. Sample the edibles during the holiday season or wait, as they did in olde England, for the Day of Epiphany to gobble up the goodies.

Cooking Up Christmas

At the time that Queen Victoria ascended to the throne (1837) a traditional Christmas dinner included roast beef (in the North of England) or goose (in the South). Other dishes might have been peacock, turtle soup, oyster patties, mashed potatoes, suckling pig, boar, port jelly, and, of course, plum pudding and mince pies.

In America, turkey was substituted for roast peacock. Ham did not replace suckling pig until the late 1800's. Back in England, roast turkey did not appear on the Royal Christmas Day 'menu until 1851.

We are including some early American recipes (cooks beware!) along with contemporary versions, to give the reader a taste of a Victorian Christmas.

41

STANDING RIB ROAST

Select a 2-rib or 3-rib standing rib roast (4 to 5 pounds). Place fat side up in roasting pan; season with salt and pepper and place in 350° oven. Do not cover and do not add water.

Allow 18 to 20 minutes per pound for rare roasts, 22 to 25 minutes per pound for medium, and 27 to 30 minutes per pound for well-done. Serve with Yorkshire Pudding.

TURKEY ROAST
(EARLY AMERICAN RECIPE)

*TO ROAST A TURKEY—Make a stuffing like that for veal;
or take a tea cup of Sausage meat and add a like quantity
of bread crumbs, with the beaten yolk of two eggs—then
fill the crop; dredge the turkey over with flour, lay it before
the fire, taking care this is most on the stuffed part, as that
requires the greatest heat. A strip of paper may be put on
the breast bone to prevent its scorching. Baste with a little
butter or salt and water at first, then with its own
drippings. A little before it is taken up, dredge it again
with flour, baste with butter and froth it up. A larger
turkey (8 lbs) requires full three hours roasting—a smaller
one in proportion. (Ham or tongue is usually eaten with
turkey; stewed cranberries also.)*

THE WAY TO LIVE WELL AND BE WELL WHILE WE LIVE,
BY MRS. S. J. HALE, 1839

ROAST TURKEY

Dress and clean turkey. Rub inside with salt and pepper. Stuff neck cavity. Fasten opening with metal pins. Fill body cavity loosely with stuffing. Rub with butter or make paste of 1/2 cup butter, 3/4 cup flour; spread over all parts of the turkey.

Place turkey breast side down in open roasting pan to allow juices to run down into breast. Drip pan from broiler may be used if large roaster is not available. Roast uncovered in 300° to 325° oven 15 to 20 minutes per pound, turning turkey over onto back when half done.

Baste at 30-minute intervals with mixture of melted butter and hot water. When breast and legs become light brown, cover with brown paper. Turkey is done when the meat pulls away from the leg-bones.

Roast Goose

Preheat oven to 450°. Clean out body cavity, remove
excess fat, wash goose in cold water and wipe dry.
Sprinkle with salt and pepper. Stuff with bread stuffing.
Place breast side up on rack in roasting pan. Prick all over
with fork. Pour 2 cups boiling water over goose and
reduce oven to 350°. Roast 25 to 30 minutes per pound.
For stuffed goose, add another 20 minutes to cooking
time. When goose is done, garnish with cranberries and
watercress, and serve with apple sauce.

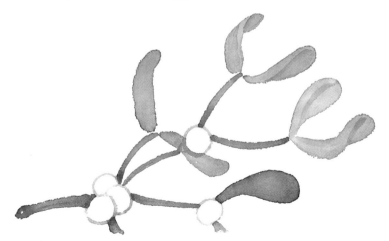

STUFFING
(EARLY AMERICAN RECIPE)

A good stuffing for veal, mutton or poultry: Take two cups of bread crumbs and one of butter or minced suet, a little parsley, finely shredded, one quarter of a nutmeg grated, a tea-spoonful of powdered lemon peel, allspice, and salt— the whole to be worked together with two or three yolks of egg, well beat.

THE WAY TO LIVE WELL AND BE WELL WHILE WE LIVE,
BY MRS. S. J. HALE, 1839

STUFFING

3/4 cup ground pork
1 tablespoon powdered sage
1 teaspoon salt
1 teaspoon pepper
3/4 cup bread crumbs (rye or whole wheat)
2 egg yolks, beaten

Blend pork, sage, salt, and pepper. Mix with bread crumbs. Add beaten egg yolks and mix thoroughly.

Baked Virginia Ham

Place ham fat side up on rack in open roasting pan. Add one-third inch water to pan. Do not cover. Bake in 350° oven, allowing 20 minutes per pound for a large ham; 25 minutes per pound for a small ham; and 30 minutes per pound for a half ham. Roast meat thermometer registers 170° when ham is done. Ham may be basted during cooking period with ginger ale or cider. For the last half hour of baking, rub surface with mustard and brown sugar. Score fat in diamonds; stick a whole clove in each.

ENGLISH PLUM PUDDING

10 slices white bread

1 cup scalded milk

1/2 cup sugar

4 eggs, separated

1-1/3 cups golden raisins, lightly floured

1/2 cup finely chopped dates

3 tablespoons finely chopped citron

3/4 cup finely chopped suet

3 tablespoons brandy (optional)

1 teaspoon nutmeg

1/2 teaspoon cinnamon

1/4 teaspoon ground cloves

1/4 teaspoon mace

1 teaspoon salt

Crumb bread and soak in hot milk. Cool and add sugar, egg yolks, raisins, dates, and citron. Cream suet in food processor and add to crumb mixture. Stir in brandy (if desired), nutmeg, cinnamon, cloves, mace, and salt. Beat until well blended. Beat egg whites until stiff but not dry. Stir a third of the egg whites into pudding mixture; gently fold in the remainder. Spoon mixture into a buttered 2-quart mold and cover. Steam for 6 hours in a large covered pot holding boiling water to come halfway up the sides of the mold. Remove and let cool for 10 minutes before unmolding. Serve with warm hard sauce.

HARD SAUCE

5 tablespoons butter
1 cup confectioners sugar
1/2 teaspoon vanilla

Cream butter, add sugar and beat with electric beater until pale and creamy. Add vanilla and blend. Cover and refrigerate until needed.

MINCE PIES
(EARLY AMERICAN RECIPE)

Ingredients for mincemeat:--One and a half pounds of lean underdone roast beef, two pounds of beef suet, one pound of stoned raisins, one pound of picked sultanas, one and a half pounds of apples, one and a half pounds of pears, one pound of mixed peel, three quarters of a pound of blanched and chopped Valencia almonds, the thin peel of two oranges and two lemons. All the before-mentioned ingredients are to be chopped and then mixed with one pound of well washed and dried currants, a quarter of an ounce of mixed powdered spice, the juice from the lemons and oranges, one and a half pounds of Demerara sugar, half a pint of brandy, half a pint of sherry, half a pint of port, one wineglassful each of Marshall's maraschino syrup and noyeau syrup, and a quarter of a pint of Silver Rays (white) rum.

Make some puff paste, roll it out a quarter of an inch thick, and line some little plain or fancy pattypans with it; place a teaspoonful or dessertspoonful, or more, of mincemeat in each, according to its size, wet the edges of the paste and cover the mincemeat over with more paste; brush over the top with beaten-up whole raw egg, and put them in a quick oven for about five minutes, then take them out, dust them over with icing sugar to glaze them, and put them back to bake for fifteen to twenty minutes. Dish up in a pile on a dishpaper or napkin, and serve hot.

FROM MRS. AGNES B. MARSHALL'S COOK BOOK
FROM THE EARLY VICTORIAN PERIOD

MINCEMEAT PIE

*1 can (1-2/3 cups) mincemeat
2 cups thin-sliced apples
1 teaspoon grated lemon peel
2 tablespoons lemon juice
Pastry for 9-inch 2-crust pie*

Combine mincemeat, apples, lemon peel, and juice; heat thoroughly. Pour into 9-inch pastry-lined pie pan; adjust top crust. Sprinkle with a small amount of sugar and bake in 400° oven 35 minutes.

There's More!

There's more, much more to Christmas
   Than candle-light and cheer;
It's the spirit of sweet friendship,
   That brightens all the year;
It's thoughtfulness and kindness,
   It's hope reborn again,
For peace, for understanding
   And for goodwill to men!

ANONYMOUS